OTHER BEASTS

Acknowledgements

Acknowledgements are due to the editors of the following publications where a number of these poems first appeared: *London Magazine, Poetry London, Poetry Review, Poetry Wales, Stand, The Rialto.*

'Killer Whales on a Beach in Fiji' and 'Bird Farm', were also published in *By Heart/Uit Het Hoofd,* in English and Dutch translation, Five Leaves Press, 2006.

'Testimony' and 'Dead Hare' were first published in *The Intelligent Woman's Guide,* University of Huddersfield press, 2007.

Thanks to Yaddo Foundation for a residency in the summer of 2005. Thanks to the Yorkshire Arts Council and The Royal Literary Fund for grants that enabled the completion of this book.

For Friends

OTHER BEASTS
Sarah Corbett

seren

Seren is the book imprint of
Poetry Wales Press Ltd.
57 Nolton Street, Bridgend, Wales, CF31 3AE
01656 663018
www.seren-books.com

ISBN 978-1-85411-466-2

A CIP record for this title is available from the British Library.

The publisher acknowledges the financial assistance of the Welsh Books Council.

Cover image: Théodore Gericault 'Cheval au Galop'
© Musées d'Art et d'Histoire de Chambéry.

Printed in Bembo by Bell & Bain, Glasgow.

Contents

Birthday

For my father on the 14th November

I go into the closing day.
A last slice of palm-tinted light
peels back off the moor.
Exposed is the hill's double-helix
as mist wells rain from the valley.
Each step is a push from the chest
and away, as far as I can get.
I can do this: run towards night,
body drawing the road's river,
body a nocturnal bloom.
It's here for the taking:
my arms open for the lift
and I'm almost into the air,
not some kind of shifting
or even the memory of a dream,
but my full, bone-heavy form
briefly allowed a miracle.
This will do. I am here for you
and nearly, nearly, it is loosed.
In the black envelope of lane
a figure waits, then a white halo:
an old man walks a dog,
a Husky that locks my gaze,
strains after the scent-shadow
anchoring a trail in my wake.
I bark, bark. Other beasts
complain back under the weight of dark.

Sky Watching

In the car at night as my father drove
us back from my grandparents' house,
I would lean my head against the window
and watch the sky unleash the long whip
of its mountains, its river's black ribbons.

The glass would be cold on my temple,
the nub of the lock pressing my shoulder,
the cold in my eyes and nose and mouth,
like waking outside in the small hours
and finding the cloud has finally cleared.

Every now and then the contour of the road
would lose us the moon; it would flip
from left to right, a child in a game.
It was as if we were not travelling at all,
but turning with it to keep our faces upturned.

Comet

I walked at night over Fountains Fell under Pen-y-Ghent.
The moor was a still wave and I was riding it,
my head capped in the sky's metal.

The god was hammering out stars, the hill its anvil.
Where they fell they left a darker trail,
the glints speeding away in the gill.

Hale-Bopp was a fist of flung glitter, a child's firework
on black paper, my marker the five miles
from dale to dale.

I never made it to the village,
but lay under the broken eaves of a barn,
watched to see the god unsheathe his sword.

Bird Farm

We lay under swifts
feasting in the fallow field.
I bathed you beneath the willow,
you were a gold button.

At dusk we called in the hens,
feral in the hazel grove.
Tipped the corn first thing,
dug for eggs in the musty beds.

You slept in the barrow,
four days cutting the yew hedge.
Last egg in the nest,
the blue unbroken one.

Odd days we climbed the hill,
past the wild gooseberries,
past the great wheat fields.
Watched the swifts ascend.

Rainbow

In the hotel room we saw the beauty of home,
too far out to touch still, and effervescently moving,
played the 'being home' game, until it felt too real,
as if I'd stepped back and left you, watering the roses.

We read until dark and Pluto winked its blue eye
behind the curtain. There was too much clear space,
and the moment panning out was like the light breaking
over the valley, the rain coming over the Sierras.

The fan turned the warm air loudly and the same bee
reconnoitred the window. A chorus of car horns
repeated after the game, and in the gaps a she-cat mouthed
the necks of her kittens as she moved them.

When you left me, turning to the wall for sleep,
I smoothed the skin of your small tanned back,
the damp crook of your leg over the covers,
your slim bruised foot crossing Russia for home.

Lights

Once up against the sky it's hard
To tell them from the stars
− 'The Armadillo', Elizabeth Bishop

In the space of a day the children
outgrow us. We try to catch them
but they have shiny new skins.
It is late when they ride past,
the lights of small fires on their faces.

In our stranger times, the lights
were ships docking from the skies.
We thought they had come to take us
and held the stones, little tugs of grief,
the earth's keepers.

We watch the steady fall of lights.
It is as if a brilliant end is in sight:
we have lit the touch papers
and are waiting for the lanterns
to burn out.

Rivers, Roads

Rivers are roads, cutting their borders.
Roads are rivers, sutures on muted greens.
Small spots are signs, circles on hills
or gradients on a frozen tarn depth rings.

Wave tips telescope; there are engine rainbows.
The end of land has been expertly carved.
Wings are joyful above snowfall cumulous
in the blue clear above the cirrus.

Pools are erasures, the creeping cars creeping,
white diagrams of houses paths for worship.
A wooded copse is a crop of hairs
dropped like aitches in the hollows.

Beauty is elicit, and the city just left
a milk-caul, frost on leaf, just that.

Seen From Above

More delicate than the historian's are the map maker's colors.
— 'The Map', Elizbeth Bishop.

The phone presses against my cheek
where it will leave a small red mark.
My hand rests on the page of a book

where earth is seen from space,
the whole fluent marble of her.

It is your spring after the rains,
the sun bloody over the veld
as dahlias breach light under the window.

Here, clear mornings mushroom into rain,
earth is a tortoise of brown and rust
shuffling into the dark.

We argue over who is up, who is down.
I cannot see my country, only a dot of cloud
pitched off the wing of a continent,

but Africa is a stamp, an emblem,
a massive elephantine head.

We are talking borders, visas, distance.
How strange we cannot simply step across
these shared phases of the moon.

Taking the Night Train

All night the train followed the Rhine.
I watched the river, an opened seam,
bend to the sway of the track,
the forest a hackle raised along its back.

Every now and then we'd leave it and enter
deep wood, a sort of muffled trap descending
like an outlaw's hand on the muzzle of a horse,
until a new turn returned us to the water's course.

Above the haar, raised and lit in staged intervals,
hung the crenellated turrets of castles,
like cut-outs you might paste to a book
and light with tissue paper in windows.

I slept in fits, caught glimpses between naps
from the snapped up screen, the rocking berth
waking me, a sea-sickness or rolling dream.
I knew the Alps were close, felt the unseen

bodies of mountains press out the dawn,
a whole village a rare night bloom
blue as first milk, hung like a lantern
in some unnamed crevice of the hills.

Pietà

You are years dead, but my dream has gathered
me up and sent me before time to look
on your death bed, a scene in old master

tints: brocade reds and vintage tarnish, book
binder's leathers; and from above
a gleam kindling souls in every nook.

I am surprised by the weight of love,
a buoyancy I ride as if a boat
and holding your hand is what a green wave

might do. You ask for light, more light.
I strip back layers from the window:
nails, sacking, boards, until a sleight

of hand lets fall bright pieces and bestows
the morning on your head. Your daughters
stand, hands folded, glossed in pinks and yellows.

Their watch approves me, my flawless
offering entering the seam and groove
of this stage lit for mortals like us.

Reversal

I get up in the mid-frame of the night
as if to go to my grandparents' room
and at the door stop and wake.

Many times I lay in the stiff high bed
where my teenage aunt had her nightmares,
pulling creatures from the patterned walls.

Nana would tighten me in to the ironed sheets
that I fought to loosen with my feet,
leave me a crack of yellow from the hall.

There was the shawl from their one trip abroad,
the moth-eaten bull with the fake blood,
the castanet carapaces that clicked,

and the wardrobe whose door wouldn't shut,
stuffed with old suits in polythene sleeves,
the mirror that showed a face if I looked.

This was my grandparents' room when I slept
in the narrow one with the purple walls,
where I was woken by a rainbow at midnight,

the fairy light of it across my bed a bridge,
and climbed downstairs in what I thought
was noon, with a blue bird singing on the sill,

entered in on a room of figures, ghosts ringed
in the smoking gloom, the green face of the TV set
gaping like their caved in mouths.

And I see it now, what I couldn't then – creeping
with fear to their bed, where they lay like tucked in
dolls in the moony glow of the curtains –

Nana's face too tight for sleep, her eyelids ridged and still,
her mouth a line pressed firmly not answering my calls.

Hearsay

They said I barked like a dog
and when tickled could stop breathing without warning.
There's a story of how I turned blue in my cot
and my father ran with me to the doctor's in the village.

I can see him, running, his face suspended in fear,
and my own breath stopped –
like coming to on the kitchen floor,
his hands about my head, his trembling, his dry tears.

What I remember is driving through woods to a house
where I threw up in a white tiled bathroom
with a porcelain bowl, and sat
in a red armchair, clammy and reeling;

the clap of my brown shoes on green lino,
the elastic tops of my white knee socks,
their criss-cross flesh marks under the cotton;
the high windows grey with mesh

and the corridor telescoped, as if I was under ether,
on the way to the X-ray
where my white chest lay beneath the machine
and two men mouthed soundlessly;

the machine for breathing kept under my bed
I have no picture for, only the hole I fell into
when they turned out the lights
and went, smoking, to their rooms.

Breaking Horses

1

My love of horses comes down
on my father's side, through his father's father.
There's a photograph, lost now too,
of the cabbie in his coat and whiskers

holding the head of a tall gelding
in its upright shoes, the tied-in fetlocks
and roughed up cannon bones
those old cab horses always seem to show.

The story goes how the old man
whipped a driver known for his cruelty,
brought him to his knees in the street,
a long flick and smack about the neck

as their cabs passed. With this for pride
I was both tethered to the post
of my ancestor and sent skittering on
like a yearling with its rump slapped.

2

My last summer at home thirteen mountain ponies were found, ruined, but still alive, in a quarry above Caerwys, their lips cut off at the teeth, their ears close to their heads, their eyelids cut to the bone, as Evnissyen did to the horses of the King of Ireland. What had they been brought to witness, these thirteen? Their fetlocks had been tied, and they lay tethered on their sides, eyes back to the white, a row of grimaces. The local news was full of it, and there was a general outcry, talk of ritual and spell, of something risen that had long lay buried.

3

Dostoevsky knew. It took three pages
to mark the death of that horse
whipped to its knees in the dream,
the small boy Raskolnikov holding
all that time his mother's hand,
this one anchor tying him to the horror,
pushing it back somewhere – into his mouth,
behind his teeth and tongue – the hungry
cells of his brain opening a snap
then shuttering on the tiny upturned picture.

I lay on my bed in the early evening,
unaware of the darkening tablet of window,
the lights flicking on a mile across the estuary
and the night birds setting out.
I read like this for weeks all summer,
and the walls held in that small room
like a drawing of a girl reading,
her mind an open mouth, an unfed hunger,
the broken horse and the inaudible snap
of the rope inside her.

My Border Ancestry

I learnt to whistle in the woods at Ewloe, my hand in my father's hand, the sound coming at first like a thrumble at the lips, more spit than song. Years later we had our one talk there, of my mother, and how he'd loved her.

I stood one twilight on a Norman mound by Offa's Dyke, the bodies of men and women lifting in the bulbous air, drifts of talk and whispers, a language I understood without understanding, a strange flame licking round us.

One day at Montgomery I heard a voice drum out and looked down to the plain below, the battle a mirage shifting up from the field. I had been there before, knew it from the nausea's sudden veil.

Another time I rose like a wraith from the grassed over courtyard at Flint, the old tongue coming back beyond what I'd ever learnt at school, throwing me like a sovereign to be wished on in the deep pool.

Our line is dying out in those border towns: the uncle with the plate in his skull, the ill fated cousins. There is a church where the last invading lords lie entombed, and a ruined manor house.

Three Ravens on a white shield mark my father's name, the name drawing itself from the beak, like the three on Long Mynd that circled, black glints up close, a ravenous shouting.

Doing the I Ching

The New Year had rung in and the city was snowbound.
We'd drunk late at a party – two friends I'd lose within the year –
slid down the packed ice of the street, felt at home and released,
though we'd agreed to go North, to where you were.

Many times I'd weighed you against other lovers, like handfuls of soil
equally dark and rough; I could have stayed then and never
set fate going. In the end it was the weather that held us,
and some unspoken sense that what was right was in balance, here.

But there was a pull stronger than our small hive of knowing,
a tribe we felt we belonged to, holding on to the celebrations
until we arrived at Billy's Cabin, a warm pocket against
the iron frosts on the hills above Loch Lomond.

We each had our own thing for divination, a consensus
for some unnamed power we could trust. Undecided,
we knelt close on the floor, made our own warmth in the cold room
over that small hard book, stacked pennies for yarrow stalks

until the patterns told in darts and chevrons how still mountains
keep no promises and the long road won't turn without us.
We had to dig out the car and push it to the junction,
but once past Leeds we were clear. I believe now

it was someone else's future I'd hitched a ride on.
When we met again and kissed that slow tongue kiss,
I knew I was taking something without permission,
and this was when, this was when the change came.

The Stoat and the Rabbit

I see us now, in the scud light of midsummer,
my belly was just pushing out my dress
and you wore that Indian shirt I liked.
We'd walked out past the university
to where parkland turned back to fen
in thin muddy streams and waist high grass.

On the way back, the light had metalled over
and the air thickened for rain. We stopped
in the quiet and the emptiness, the dull presence
that seemed to rise between us at times like this,
when something raced from the line of trees
we'd kept as markers to our left.

There were sparks off the tall grass, close up in a rush,
the blood rush after a head stand or near miss.
An under-the-breath tonguing tied slipknots
our feet kept slipping as the chase climaxed,
its hissing sound trail headlights at night,
the last shout caught on camera like pain on the retina.

Fox at Midnight

It is the longest night and we are out,
crossing the field from the house.
Our shadows fall through the trees like owls.

A fox slips from the wood. It has come
for the sheep lain dead for days by the well.
We stop. It is thin, its red dips

to blood red at its ribs, a vixen
in its fluid line and lightness
with cubs to feed, scurried under the earth.

She comes swiftly on and begins to dance,
throwing the sheep's mantle
like a crown of blossom over her back,

pirouetting neatly in the last of the guts.

Dream House

Just the same, I saw it, striking
from two pines, limbs
bent to the sky.
Closer, it was a ruined house,

like the one we came to that night
after our long journey –
before it fell, before the dust raised
the mountains around us.

The house had eyes like owls,
a child's bike on the drive,
and there was a movement of sea
where the dirtied fields dropped down.

It lived up to nothing –
an unfolding box of dark rooms,
spirograph of corridors, and only,
far from the smell,

a chamber like an afterthought,
like the glassed-in hideouts
in Jacobean houses.
It stays with me – the way we moved

space by space, arbiters of the dream,
hands on the wall, like feeling
for something still going,
or angry,
that could move us.

Stained Glass

If only light dropped auroras to glaze her hands,

and then, there she is, before the window,
a woman in blues and violets.

There is gold, and the day glancing through,

in her arms a lyre,
or a book, a song anyway, rivulets of warmth,
water refracted onto her face.

★

The phone rings. Light closes.
A dream re-inserts itself:

a table, a book,
a dowsed candle, weltered, worn down,
slip-shod at the sides.

She reaches for the book,
fingers the edge, the caul of the page.

A poem lifts off, somehow known –
on the hill that time.

★

Cold steps in, the room greys.
She is tide bound, end stopped, a broken line.

If only something would take her –
a terrible illness, weeks with nothing
but the movement of clouds, the light palette.

★

The machine clicks, records.
She moves outside: winter greens,
on the sill a small bird.

Last night a strangeness in the sky –
snowbanks, a diffuse moon –
shining, as through skin.

Now dark cumulous, a horizon of hills,
earth glow off the rim.

You Said Something

She sat up late after washing the kitchen floor,
listening to Polly Jean, drifting off into herself,
clean, relieved of a task.

How she hates the housework –
like polishing up the bars of a cage,
like making hell smell fresh,

but that night it contained its own achievement,
the cleared surfaces creating enough light
to feel by, a sense she rarely touched these days.

For a moment she stepped into the night –
it was raining lightly and the dark was painting with it –
walked her wet footprints on to the still damp floor.

Three Slipped Lives

after the Photographs of Jeff Wall

1. Insomnia

He lies under the table by the fridge,
his blanket the shadows, his pillow a fist.

The all-night light dubs the window velvet,
and the wall outside makes bars of it.

We are pressed inside,
close enough to the blue bulb of his foot,

the floor tiles furred like an animal
severed from its skin.

There is a vertical slit from the broom cupboard,
a black line of escape;

from this angle he wouldn't fit.

2. Odradek

In the shadow in the hall sits the stool
with the slit seat, its wound of yellow foam,
that makes her think of the doll

she hid each night under her mess of clothes,
its scrubbing brush hair,
the painted eyes that couldn't close.

The pay phone clings to the wall.
She lives on the top floor, too far
to reach the calls of friends who fail to call,

or ring and stir the old man, her neighbour,
who seems to listen for her footfall
and looks out, pensive, as she pauses on the stairs.

3. Forest

The light is a green dusk you have just lit.
We almost see the brown arm of your jacket,

a lifted plimsoll, its sole smudging the edge.
There is a stove, canister of gas, kettle, cups,

a wrapped up bundle, gathered sticks,
like the prize in a maze, or the inside

of a dream house where we are guests,
you the keeper or gingerbread witch.

And here you live, an outsized bird
vanished to the cul-de-sac in the woods,

dropping back when we're done
to peck at crusts dropped from our pockets.

Buried Reindeer

For Zac Solomons

There are buried reindeer, known only by their antlers in the frozen grass.
Life is like that – we see what gleams in the frost light under the clear night;

and their bodies pant hotly in the earth beneath us as we pass.

There are these hours etched on a window blacked up with fire or the grime
of years, like the nail marks of someone trying to get out or look in,
like the scratched-in winter in the blacked-up wood on the woodcut's
                                                    master copy.

There is the turn in the lane that signals the return, as far as we go then,
and back to the lights and warmth and click of time. We talk of

what is lost and gained, how far you can go with a stranger.

We step against the moon, play it out as an illusion, sliding the shadows
from our shoes as if we can never have been there, to know it and not return –

the way we'd see things – the perfect body of a tree and its other in ice
                                                    traced over it.

Where does it go, all that beauty – pausing on a stepping stone to look
                                                    at a river,
one body protecting another, the sky swallowed down there,
between the rocks where the water slips? Bridges, and other things,

like steps out of stone wedged into mud or water to let us cross.

The Children in the Attic

We climbed there from our cold white bedroom,
the youngest legged up first, a child ghost,
his nightshirt billowing out,

stayed a day or two, away from the shouting,
quartered like a small troop of way-laid soldiers.

There was a rusted spindle, a laundry press,
a folded iron bedstead,
forgotten things long shoved from sight;
and a ruby window set well under the eaves
that turned our hands to thieves' hands.

The air was dry and hot, as if some big mouth
had sucked all the damp out
and the only light came along the cobwebbed
pathways of shadows.

It was like a dream, the way we left,
slipping into a grainy dawn,
picking our way along the roof's ridge
then stepping off,
and, instead of falling, landing somewhere
faintly familiar

but ruined – the other of home, its skeleton.

Man with Knives

From his shirt back
slips ivory handled
a slick fish slice,

from under his collar
a leaf fall of razors;
sleeves relinquish silver

seed spinners
and a sickle blade
the size of a crow feather

or a lion's claw.
He shows me this,
how easily he could fillet me.

The only thing is to move
in close to his mouth
that is a precise

lathe curvature, his naked
torso planed smooth
as the breast of Bucephalus,

and taking his breath
in my mouth-scabbard,
glide the twin carvers

from his hip pockets.
He is laughing now,
clatter of sharps, a rain

of piercings, gives up
his feet to my thumb's pumice,
my hand's tannery –

from each sole a fall
of tiny gold daggers.

Kisses

They are a kiss just in the way they stand.
He leans softly in to her; they have that look.
He holds his first decade in his hands
like his awareness of her, her small heat.

In the next frame they have turned to kiss,
the boy's black hair a scruff in her fist
as she holds him to her. There is intimation
of tongues, of give, and something fiercer.

There is innocence in this, an untaught wisdom,
a curdled-down riff in the pit of it,
a beetle brilliance that catches us once in its heat
as children taking our first kiss.

In the alley by your grandmother's house
he held you to the wall; his mouth, open-lipped
on yours, tongued the gaps. You recall
the pressing heat of his breast, a faint tinge

of urine on his breath, the kissing
of legs as he lifted your yellow dress.

The Dog's Kiss

It's an old memory, the one
I have of the girl, her father
and their dog – a white English Bull
with a blue eye

pink-rimmed, a pirate's patch, paper
hats for ears. It lay on its back
on the kitchen table, eight black
studs for nipples

and a stitched seam for its navel,
its tongue the flat end of a flecked
purple tie in the father's hand,
whose bald head bent

to the domed chest. For a moment
he looked to be strangling it,
then his hand moved and covered the
slug black muzzle

as you might a small, stunned creature –
with gentle hand – not mortal fight,
but, his mouth stretched over the dog's
mouth, mortal kiss.

Minutes earlier, it had hung –
a fish lifted from a river,
a plumb at the end of its line –
on the yard door.

It had leapt for a fox that stuck
its snout under the crack to where
the dog slept on its short rope,
left its freedom.

Swinging then, its body softened
into the fall, its paws up-curled –
like being born, like being rubbed –
was how he found it,

turning back on his outward path
for his wallet and smokes.
He'd taken up that dumb weight
as his own weight,

the weight of his heart, left his mouth.
The dog lay, weighted with his grief.
Wet glistened on his cheeks, his eyes
falls of cut glass

as he drew back, looked up, and spat
a long finger of saliva
on the floor. Only us two, just
at the door, saw

the dog leap and aerial twist,
like its nemesis the cat, and
righting itself in mid-air, land
square, on all fours.

Mountain Pony

After the auction, he entered the pen.
His fifty guinea colt pressed its hide
of beaten silver to the bars,
as if to disassemble and return

to be made whole under the stars
and the mauve hills. But the signal
of winter was in the dung and death smell,
the steel and mortar of the sale yard.

He sat in one corner, made no move
or voice, but a ring of still flutterings,
waited for the rich soundings
of the animal's heart and breath to come.

Night had fallen in at the iron roof
by the time it had settled, hoof by hoof
finding purchase on the concrete floor
for the bird of its fear.

Killer Whales on a Beach in Fiji

We watered them, the whole night their backs
caught the light of our flares and shimmered.
We sheathed them in towels, sheets from our beds,
half the town midwife to these ocean offspring,
lost, or some envoy of the lost.

When the tide rose to meet us, we held them
in the shallows, great buoys taking their weight
against ours, our thighs strained forward,
our feet grounded in their sand replicas.
A pulse echoed back and forth between them.

For hours their strength gathered, collectively:
when one moved, they all moved, a swell in the wave
lifting them from our hands, rocking us away.
We kept a vigil, lit fires along the shore,
spirit chasers, keeping the boundary intact between worlds,

heard their song, out there, where the ocean pounded,
like a drum we'd made between us
slipping whole from the darks' mouth.

Watching *The Company of Wolves*

– after Angela Carter & Neil Jordan; for Gabrielle

The wolf girl climbs from the well,
naked but for her spine's mat of hair.
She is drawn by the heat of the village,
her homage at the turn of winter.

They may keep a fragment of her here,
in this yellow lamp against the window,
a half buried hope against hope after a long war
or simply the abandoned light of her.

An obtuse moon makes strange the trees
and strange the river under the bridge,
eating what music plays for the scene;
clouds are a platoon of sky ships.

Outside this room an old war resumes.
The picture will crack as we watch,
a seal breaking on another darkness,
the image stay in our minds as a still.

Mother and The Bomb

Mother in her polka dot dress
waits for the bus to light the corner to town.
She laughs, holds her hair down against the wind,
thinks of last night's kiss.

They talk of sex, now they are women,
and the garter pinches their thigh's white fat,
the pad leaks more often than not,
and the smell is new and they are open.

But they are half-women and don't know yet
how they will fuck and come and love it,
like their mothers and their grandmothers.
It's all smoothed over still, shiny and wet.

Their bodies turn, blind and specific
and the world pauses at this moment
as they shelter from the rain,
awaits Krushchev's turn in the Atlantic.

Years later, we are at the same stop,
the ghost print of her belted mac against the red bus.
How wide the gap from pavement to step
and stepping in, how we vanished.

Dreaming History

There was a long drive that day. We stopped for fuel
and toffee popcorn, shared in handfuls on the way home.
The red pick-up was filmy from the road, and it was hot,

so hot the cab exhumed heat like dust from a broken down
vacuum, the one mama pushed over the hall carpet.
We hung our heads out the window as the dog lolled his tongue.

I was upstairs sleeping when they came. That's how I made it.
The youngest, I'd been shown how to fit the catch
of the rosewood trunk so as to breathe and not get stuck.

We all knew it was a matter of time. The two hired lads
kept their rifles cocked and loaded. In the end they were undone
like a couple of jack rabbits enjoying the last of the sun.

Papa took a bullet to his head from the back. My brothers
they hung from the turkey oak in the kitchen garden. Mama,
and the maid. Well, you can guess at that. The dog went to poison,

snuffing out a vixen trail in the orchard. I heard it all – Mama's
high black heels that clacked then stopped, the tea tray's crash,
the maid's prayer from the scullery cupboard.

I lay tight as a nut in the musk of out-of-season dresses,
thought of the moth bound under the sill in its wrap
of candy floss, how I liked to poke it out onto the grass

and see the half-made creature gasp. After, came the quiet,
and I must have slept, because I remember holding to the sway
top of a pine, the resin running sweeter and sweeter on my hands,

just my weight bending the tree, no wind, the quiet, and the way
I knew I'd always now be alone. Our own militia found me, farmers
forced to take up arms. They set me on our old knock-kneed donkey

who'd been grazing peacefully by the river, said it was clear to the
                                                                border.

Testimony

I.

I remember dust and the road a parched tongue pushing,
far as I could see, to an orange merge with a deadpan sky
grey in the heat haze; and crickets kicking off their crazed
fantasia as the sun began to drop and fizz-up the west.

I knelt by the roadside in my sweat-cracked T-shirt, goosed-up
despite the heat, watched the tracks to the horizon.
There was a darkened blur on the dirt that changed as the light
changed to one of those passion faces, dog-eyed and mournful.

I'd lain for hours in the grass, hardly allowing my breath –
hardly believing they wouldn't come back – lain flat as a snake,
only my eyes moving, back and forth, my ears pricking
at the silence blooming around me, the day thinning out.

I'd let two trucks pass for the fear in me, but knew I'd have to move
before nightfall and raise the alarm. So when a white pick-up
ghosted the distance and I saw a woman's blond fall of hair,
I raised my arm and crawled, calling, forgetting I could walk.

2.

I knew I was a goner by the blue horses.
Neat and lithe they were, perfect
pygmy replicas a solid ultra-
marine. They looked up from their grazing
among the ordinary horses

as I left by the hole in my chest.
I didn't feel the shot, only an implosion
of light and a sucking force,
like my grandmother drawing the fire
with an opened sheaf of newspaper,

the grandmother who went of cancer,
saying, don't be afraid, there's nothing to fear;
and I felt nothing, looking back
at my body on the road, watching
the dust darkening with my blood.

3.

They took me back there, had me tell the whole thing again to get it clear.
I kept retreating on myself, reaching for a beginning: the slowing of the beat
up blue truck and the way the door opened as the arm disappeared,

the last lift that took us as far as the gas station and had us walking to the turn,
then the draw of the desert road, how we got that far, you with your daft songs
and military steps, of drinking the blood of wallabies if we went bush,

the fight at Alice Springs where you said I never got the heart of things,
or when you picked me up from town that day in your father's car
and I felt the back of your hand against my knee as you shifted gear.

My story ran in circles like a dog at its tail. I was still under the thrall
of my fugitive hours, whether it was luck or grace, like grandpa in the war,
the gift of his luck in slipping from under that particular day's horror.

And I knew they didn't believe me. Their sun-dark faces showed
a kind of fear, as if I'd come out of the belly of the place itself.
They kept me two days in a cell when I was desperate for home, for you,

anything but here. It was weeks before they traced us back to that last hotel,
then, god knows, dug up my one, brief infidelity. They made me go
when my visa was up, convinced you'd turn up whole on some distant coast.

4.

Things came back, not my whole
life but scenes, only keener,
as if someone had put a pile of edits
together and rolled them backwards;
at some point, I knew
I could expect the beginning. First,
the cow shit still drying
on the blue truck's belly as it pulled up,
the way he stepped round from the passenger
side, lifted his rifle to his chest
and set his eye to the sights
as if I were no more than a bird
or troublesome beast;
then the shining hub of your hair
turned around my hand and
the arch of your back, the filter
of the cheap red curtains plastering the wall
as we lay drowning in the heat
of that last hotel; diving
off coral reef into rainbow
hoards of fish that nipped our backs,
the tiger sharks nosing by, the waterfall
of sunlight that caught me off guard;
out with my younger brother in an electrical storm
the weekend before we left, the hard
silver of the strike on the horizon,
his girlfriend's pregnancy
a conjoined joy between us;
my father's death. My father's death
and my mother's face the day we buried him,
as if she'd received some kind of grace.
His taking each of our trembling hands
in his paper cool fingers
on the white of the hospital sheet.
From there the reel gathered speed,
shots flicked past until, too soon,
I was five years old
and I'd done something terribly wrong.

My heart felt as if it was turning out
on the kitchen floor all the bad thoughts
I'd ever thought, and I recognised it
as a feeling I'd carried always.
Then, in some solemn reversal
of the order of things, I turned back
to the wall where the house-martin
had made its nest, hidden
by a screen of twigs and naps of hair,
my small hands a pair of warm pale wings
held against the weavings to prevent their fall.

5.

We raised the money to come back, me and your shell-shocked mother.
She didn't want to believe me either, and I don't blame her.

We planned a private prosecution, but the police reopened the investigation.
What convinced them I can't tell beyond my determined return.

At home, in England, I'd been numb, unable to sleep, spent the winter
nights rehashing my undergraduate law. Back here I began to remember,

crashing into pits of half-conscious slumber where I dreamt, or re-lived
every broken down beat of those few minutes. The two men reared

like twin leviathans at the end of my bed, as if they had died
and had something to reveal. And I was sure for the first time

of eye colour and the faces lines, height, estimated age and weight,
the way the one man's nose knocked sideways as if broken and healed

and a left wall-eye that seemed to leer at me as he squeezed the trigger,
clear he already had his mind on the main plan;

the bitten down fingernails of the other, sore looking and close to,
the burn or scar on the paler underside of his forearm, risen and smooth

that meant we got them in the end, that was the last thing I saw
as I twisted and tore myself free from his grip in my hair

taking the next step into air, suspended for a moment like a hand puppet
dancing the back of a chair, until a force made me hit ground and run.

Thinking back, what I'd thought my own heart kicking in was the thump
as they slung you into the rear of the truck like a slain deer.

6

Reliquaries of skillet and cup
shaved to glints where the spade
sliced and razed,

a cotton dress folded back
and back on itself
like a mushroom frill.

Deeper, you'd expect bones,
flints, but nothing,
just earth darker and dampened,

even a peaty seam.
He'd have touched rock,
or core, if his friend

hadn't put his hand
on his arm, said gently,
enough, as if it was his grief

he was burying, not his crime.
An ancestor had dwelled here,
so maybe this conferred

on his mind some kind
of secondhand grace
as the figure dropped,

wrapped in a pale sheet
and bound with rope skeins
neat as observance, neat

as the dark seeps at mouth gape
and heart. A tree
flinched as a stray wind hit,

and high up a cloud joined its grove.
Way out across the plain
the dust held its tongue.

Cuttings

Monday

Invaders shoot at stars; man, lost, plays
Mozart. We will be marked, my iris'

duplicate. There are five hundred dead; for
five hundred feet a woman falls. His eyes

were dark pools from days under water
says the father of his surviving son.

Elders discuss the plight of doves; they turn,
arrays of light. In Uong Bi, blossom falls

on the heads of chickens, the few that remain.
Rain hesitates, throws beads at the window.

Tuesday

Twin feels pain as plane goes down.
In Chang Mai, bomb goes off in mosque.

Travellers tire of crying; five killed
in church by lightning. Students come

to pick flowers. We can hardly believe
we're here, says the showgirl on tour. Uncovered,

the smallness of the philosopher's eyes.
Dog walker killed by cable in storm.

In the dream again, the lost girl-child.
Confetti of starlings, rain rushing the clouds.

Wednesday

Model loses million. In Andijan fifteen
face death for protest. Man blazes

from belly of tank. We have moved from order
to chaos, says the cleric. Bombers stage

a dry run; the captured are photographed. We
will fly faster if we hum, a harmony

of coloured glass like eye pieces in dreams,
a love letter from one artist to another.

Today the jurors will visit the bay
as the winds spin closer and stronger.

Thursday

The gathering explodes. In Khadimya, heads
fall into fire and dust and darkness.

Medium finds daughter in lake. I hesitate
to believe in voices, says the mother

of the rainy night when she vanished.
On the northern shore, the beach

is but a field of blasted trees, twenty-
three of them. We will place a star in space,

a kohl-rimmed eye to look out for us. Sun
extends its season, steams rain from the road.

Friday

Frame of leaf as one man shoots
and another falls. Dream of massacre:

survivor in the crown of a bowing poplar.
The killers walked freely among us, women

scatter the seeds of their children.
In Duekuoe, villagers take flight, tools

buckled to the abandoned fields.
What fun they had, those two, their bus

grounding in the hearth of the outback.
Eyes distend in the pollinated wind

Saturday

A tyrant bears his underwear, white rag at a cell
door. At the centre of the eye, revolutions

of a song. The kids are feral, breeding guns
in the brick piles of cul-de-sacs. He might

have had time to turn his head, witness the lava's
implicit arrival. A man dreams explosions

in slow motion, glinting arc of imploding windows.
In Bolotnikovo a lake disappears. Villagers

gather carp's last silver from the split basin.
A storm cracks its knuckles over the hill.

Sunday

The blood of the living unlocks the past;
world's oldest mother gives birth to twins.

At the beginning of Eid the dictator hangs,
by nightfall, seventy are dead. We all just prayed

as the waves got higher, says the survivor
who clung to boards. In Noida province

they find fifteen skulls. The reactors
have had their day; their fortress fell

without a shot. A dream wakes us, red eye
in the dark. The sky clears for one brief hour.

Shantih

This is what I have:
scraps of belief I can no longer hold to, a dancing god
that is not my own bending me to the mat; the square
of light at midnight.

Dream of a temple filled with smaller temples
built from matchboxes;
dream of a yellow bird
slowly picking its way around the window for an exit.

Dead Hare

In the lane this morning,
a sack, daubed and wet,
like a thing drowned
and the smell that signals it –
caustic and almost tender.

I pull you back, my hand
holding you to look.
It is massed with tiny movements,
maggots, an unranked mob
working what is left –

the bunched racer's paw
on one long-hocked leg, tendon
slung over the joint,
the ear a folded tongue
against the gape of the skull.

After a pause, we walk on.
The bell rings for school
and we're going to be late.
Crows gang up ahead;
death glistens in the ditch.

Saving the Centaurs from Dante's Hell

And 'twixt the bank and it came centaurs racing
By one and one, their bows and quivers bearing
As when through the woods of the world they went a-chasing.

Canto XII, Hell

Pity Nessus, carrying the poet who sat skittishly,
dug in his heels, hitched his robes from the mess.
The blood streamed, whorled about his flanks,
congealed to tumours as he hit the bank, hauled
his bulk and almost stumbled on the slippery ground,
whereat the poet gasped at the rivulet of hair
feathering all down his human back.
Nessus could not suppress a shudder at the touch.

Behind them the river ran on, the blood and cursing,
the river of blood, the dead returned to dying. The bodies
rose and fell, twisted in the eddies and the swell,
each head surfacing seared of skin and suppurating,
to be grafted, cooled, and pulled under again. God
was hiding behind his hands up in the other sky,
where the white clouds hung like painted bells
and the angels held on, singing. This is not eternal;

the poet put you here, looking for a place
for everything in a universe sealed like a ball.
You could hoof at the sky – its lining blow to ashes,
ride out to the glade you've dreamt of in your million
dreams underground. There, rhododendron leaves
are the forest dogs' green tongues. It has just rained,
and the glisten drops like sap from the branches
and the scent comes flying over the bracken.

Save your race and your pagan hearts; we humans
need the betwixt and between, the half of the beast
that would shake the earth in the throes of love
and call us back to the gods of earth who were our
first gods. The tramping of hooves in the mossy turf,
the jostle of shoulders and swift starts,
the breath coiling, the arc over arc of necks,
the long ears flicking, the long ears flicking.

Lightning

For Jess Penrose

We look west to an armoured sky,
horizon compressed under burnt clouds.
Will it reach us? Our legs are scented
in the charcoal stubs of heather.

Then it comes: rain making cloth skin
in seconds, mouthing how hard, how cold
as we run, targets on open moorland
as the ground rises to the sky's nerve.

Safe, we spill stories: the woman
in Kansas healed as she washed her hands,
a direct hit ribbonning water
into electricity. Two Japanese girls

out in an English storm, red earth
a blue strike, the woods an X-ray,
found next morning under the tallest tree,
a puzzle in each other's arms.

Mary on the Shore

A sort of spell surrounded us... – Mary Shelley

When I see Mary
she is already in mourning,
her un-dead babies
on their umbilical knots
a crown of horrors;
the mnemonic

of her constant hands.

Shelley has been gone a day.
The wind took him
and his companions,
blowing cuts of lapis
and rough quartz
from the bay,

bringing on the darkening.

The storm gathers
the petrels before it.
They ride over the waters,
the black sky
carried on their backs
to the heads of the sailors,

like doom caps.

The friends find solace
in the white capes
of the wild riders
on their foamy mounts,
their hooves
a pleading of hands,

their hooves the ringing of bells,

a note that catches Mary
like the peculiar note
of missing
in the heart's echo-drum;
and a small blue bird,
like a daylight star,

drops from the sun.

Crow Breakfast

There is a house on a hill
you can see right through
in certain lights. It has made
a frame for the sky.

The woman who lives there
stands with both doors open
on clear nights, looking
both ways for an exit.

Birds mistake the twin
picture windows for a shortcut,
taking the mutable flight path
she cleans to a whistle.

She keeps a cemetery for the small
ones that don't make it –
what the cat doesn't destroy –
foot-clasps, a finger of feathers.

A crow once left an eye,
looking in on breakfast.

Nocturne

The house was a night house,
morning never arrived there.
Even the moon lapsed into darkness.
We stirred to its private lustre.

I had come to feed the rabbits.
It had been a long time and I was afraid –
their bead-berry eyes,
their paws at the wire.

You were there, but hid your face,
your voice a black ribbon
through the trees where you
came at last in the owl light,

your body a luminous whole,
your two hands lamps, your eyes
the tinder of something beginning,
something ending.

The house unfolds now, a box
undoing itself, the doorway
a bracelet of light we step from
into nebulae, into a dark river.